J. B. Solomon

Thoughts on Divine Inspiration

J. B. Solomon

Thoughts on Divine Inspiration

ISBN/EAN: 9783337182205

Printed in Europe, USA, Canada, Australia, Japan

Cover: Foto ©Lupo / pixelio.de

More available books at **www.hansebooks.com**

THOUGHTS

ON

DIVINE INSPIRATION.

BY

REV. J. B. SOLOMON, A.M., D.D.,

WITH AN

INTRODUCTION

BY

PROF. WHITSITT, D.D.,

Of the Southern Baptist Theological Seminary, Louisville, Ky.

Printed and Published by

BAPTIST BOOK CONCERN,

LOUISVILLE, KY.

1894.

DEDICATION.

TO HER
WHO, FOR FORTY-
FIVE YEARS, HAS BEEN MY
COMFORTER IN SORROW, MY SAFE
COUNSELOR IN TIMES OF DOUBT, MY PART-
NER IN JOY, MY SOLACE IN AFFLICTION; AND IS NOW
MY STAY IN MY DECLINING YEARS—MY WIFE—
THE FOLLOWING PAGES ARE AFFEC-
TIONATELY INSCRIBED BY
HER DEVOTED
HUSBAND.

PREFACE.

In sending forth this little treatise I would offer a word of explanation. Many valuable treatises have already been given to the world on the subject treated in the following pages. And it may seem presumptuous for one "unknown to fame" to offer anything to the reading public on a subject that has been so well discussed by abler men. My apology is found in the fact that those treatises that have fallen into my hands, at least, seem to me too scholarly for the average reader—that class that most needs a defence of the doctrines herein stated. It is for the benefit of this class more especially that this tract is given to the world. I have confined myself to very narrow limits while I have been strongly tempted to a more general discussion of the subject.

Praying that God may use it to His glory in the confirmation of the faith of His people in His divine Word, I send it forth upon its mission.

THE AUTHOR.

INTRODUCTION.

I have found much satisfaction and profit in perusing the valuable treatise which follows. The learned author has brought the public under renewed obligations by calling attention to a topic that cannot be too earnestly considered. I believe that every reader must be impressed as I have been by the admirable fitness and clearness of the arrangement. His main contention is that the harmony of teaching in the sixty-six books of the Bible, notwithstanding the fact that the authors of them lived in different ages and countries, under very diverse conditions, social, intellectual and moral, can only be explained by their being directed in thought and preserved from error by Divine Inspiration. The conception is ingenious and valuable, and it has been worked out with much patience and skill. The treatment is practical and devout. Under the influences of the Holy Spirit it cannot fail to produce excellent results. I sincerely hope that the book may be received with favor, finding attentive readers in many sections of the country.

WM. H. WHITSITT.

Southern Baptist Theological Seminary,
Louisville, Ky., July 27, 1894.

THOUGHTS ON INSPIRATION.

CHAPTER I.

INSPIRATION: WHAT IS IT?

MUCH has been written on this subject by both friends and foes, and, no doubt, much more will be written. Whether an entire agreement, in many of the phases of the questions involved, will ever be reached even by those who hold the writings of the Bible to be the inspired Word of God, may be adjourned to the decision of the future. There are doubtless many discoveries yet to be made which will have important bearings on some of the questions now under discussion. The last half century has been prolific in bringing to light many records of long past ages, and the end is not yet. But, however that may be, there are clearly differences of views among Christian scholars of to-day, as to the *nature* and the *extent* of the inspiration of the sacred Books which constitute our Bible. But while these differences may be more of less important, varying from some that are radical to those that are of a mere speculative character, and, therefore of very minor importance, yet there is a universal consensus of opinion among them that God has given to man a supernatural Revelation of Himself and His government over the world, with all that this involves; and has inspired certain of His servants to make such records of these facts as He saw fit to make known to men; and that the Bible contains these records.

But may not these differences exist, or, at least, may they not be greatly magnified in some instances, simply by the difference of terms used by different writers? In other words, may there not be less diversity of opinion respecting the *doctrine*, its nature and extent, than the terms employed by different writers would seem to indicate? And when we consider the diversities in modes of expression by different men, when the thoughts are identical, may there not be room for doubt as to whether the differences among those who accept the Bible as containing a revelation from God, and as written by inspiration, are not unduly magnified?

It is well, therefore, for us, first of all, to enquire

WHAT IS INSPIRATION

as we use the term in reference to the claims of the Bible as a Book of divine Inspiration?

Inspiration is not Revelation.—This all who have studied the matter will admit, at least in theory. And yet I have noticed that, in many instances, writers who recognize a difference of signification in the two terms, not infrequently use them as synonymous, and thus, confounding things that differ, fall into error.

It is quite true that Revelation and Inspiration are often found co-existent in the writers of the Bible, but that fact does not make them identical. As an illustration: Events which were, at the time, in the remote future, were *revealed* to Isaiah and the other prophets whose writings have been handed down to us, and they were *inspired* to announce or put them on record for the benefit of men. But the revelation and the inspiration to announce or publish the revelation were different acts of the Holy Spirit exercised upon the same individual.

It may be difficult for us to conceive of a supernatural *Revelation* unaccompanied by supernatural Inspiration, and yet this is not only possible, but has been an absolute fact in a number of instances recorded in the Bible. A striking instance of this kind is seen in the case of the servant of Elisha at Dothan. When he went out early in the morning, he beheld the city entirely surrounded by the Syrian army, which had been sent there by the King to capture Elisha, and, badly alarmed, he cried out: "Alas, my master, what shall we do?" After assuring his servant that there were more with them than with the Syrians, Elisha prayed the Lord to open his servant's eyes that he might see. The Lord answered his prayer, and opened the eyes of the young man, and "He saw: and, behold the mountain was full of horses and chariots of fire round about Elisha." (II Ki. 6:17.) Here was a supernatural Revelation, but we have no evidence that the young man was ever the subject of any supernatural Inspiration of the Holy Spirit.

A similar instance of a revelation without inspiration is found in Pharaoh's dreams which were interpreted by Joseph, who said to Pharaoh: "GOD hath SHOWED Pharaoh what He is about to do." (Gen. 41:25.) Other similar instances of divine Revelations without divine Inspiration will occur to the mind of the reader, but these will suffice for the present purpose.

In the case of Elisha's servant there was no revelation of any *future* event, but simply of a *present fact*. Yet such was its nature that he could not have known the fact in the case without the aid of supernatural power. His eyes were, in some sense, so "opened" that he could see what was invisible to his natural power of vision.

In the case of Pharaoh, a revelation was made to him of future events, through his dream, and the divinely inspired Joseph told him that the "Lord had shown him (Pharaoh) what He was about to do." In other words: God had revealed to him events yet *future*. And yet neither was Pharaoh inspired. Pharaoh received the revelation, but Joseph was the inspired interpreter of the symbols employed of God in making known His purposes. Neither Elisha's servant nor Pharaoh was inspired.

That there may be inspiration without revelation is, I think, beyond question. In fact, the larger portion of the contents of the Bible belongs to this class. All the *historical* portions of the Bible are *inspired* writings, but surely they are not all to be classed with supernatural Revelations. God never performs a useless or an unnecessary *miracle.* And what need could there have been of a *Revelation* to inform the historian of facts which he knew in the natural course of things, or with which he was personally *identified*? or of which he was "*magna pars*?" and of which he was, from the natural order of events fully *cognizant*? As illustration: What necessity was there for a supernatural Revelation to teach Moses that he had been brought up in Pharaoh's court as the adopted son of the Princess? or that he had killed an Egyptian? or that he had dwelt in Midian? or that he saw the "Burning bush?" etc., etc. All these things, nay, all the facts of his eventful life, after he reached the age of their intelligent recognition were matters of his individual personal conscious experience and observation in regard to which no supernatural Revelation was needed. He only needed the *inspiration* of the Spirit of God to prompt him to *put the facts of his life on record*, and to *guide* him in doing so—thus guarding him against mistake or forgetfulness.

But when he was called to enter upon the great work of his life, for which God had designed him (though he had not known it until God *revealed* it to him) the deliverance of his people from Egyptian bondage, the promulgation of laws for their government both civil and religious, and the leading of the Israelites through the wilderness to Canaan, he needed not only *Inspiration*, but also *Revelation*, and this was given him. And the same may be said of many other historical parts of the Bible.

The facts related in the first three chapters of Genesis were necessarily made known to man by *Revelation* only.

Striking illustrations of this view are found in the narratives of the four Evangelists—Matthew, Mark, Luke and John. They contain accounts of the life and teachings of our Lord, as witnesses of the things they record, or as having knowledge of them through entirely trustworthy witnesses. This fact is clearly stated in the first four verses of Luke's gospel, which he afterward called his "treatise." (See

Acts 1:1.) This statement is so important in this connection that I quote it in full. He writes: "Forasmuch as many have taken in hand to set forth in order a declaration (narrative) of those things which are most surely believed among us, even as they delivered them unto us, which from the beginning were eyewitnesses, and ministers of the Word; it seemed good to me also, having had perfect understanding of all things from the very first, to write unto thee in order, most excellent Theophilus, that thou mightest know the certainty of those things wherein thou hast been instructed." (See Luke 1:1–4.)

Of this language several things are worthy of special note, among them are the following:

(1) Luke makes no reference to any supernatural revelation which he had received, and his silence on the subject is *prima facie* evidence that he had not received any such revelation. (2) Neither does he lay any claim to divine Inspiration in the composition of his "Treatise." He simply says: "It seemed good to me," i. e., It seemed to me to be proper—right—that I should write an account of the life and teachings of Jesus of Nazareth.

(3) He does not claim ever to have seen Jesus, or to have heard Him speak. Nor is it very probable he ever had. But he had derived the knowledge of all he wrote concerning Jesus from others who had been "eye-witnesses, and ministers of the Word"—perfectly trustworthy sources. Luke had derived his information from more than one eye-witness, how many we do not know, and he writes his narrative from information thus obtained.

And yet *every word of our Holy Scriptures was written by inspiration of the Holy Spirit of God.* It was by this divine impulse, this moving of the Holy Spirit, upon the hearts and minds of men, that these Sacred Records were made. Whether the writers realized this fact at the time—whether they were conscious that the Spirit was using and directing them, or whether they wrote as of their own wills, irrespective of divine influences impelling and guiding them to do what they did, *does not matter.* I apprehend it might have been said of most if not all of these historians: "Ye know not what spirit ye are of." What man lives to-day who can, with confidence, claim to be able to trace the impulses which give direction to his life to their primal source? From the very nature and constitution of man, there does not live one who can do so.

So far, then, as our sacred historians knew they, most probably, wrote as simple individuals who felt an interest in the matters of which they wrote and wished to transmit a knowledge of them to posterity, while they were at the same time completely under the control of that invisible and unrecognized Power—the Holy Spirit of God. He used them as He has many a man, who knew no supreme God in the matter, unwittingly to do His will—notably, Cyrus. "All Scripture is given by inspiration of God," etc. (II Tim. 3:16.) "Holy men of God spake as they were moved (impelled, guided,) by the Holy Ghost." (II Pet. 1:21). To the same purport our Lord said to His disciples. "But the Comforter (Advocate), which is the Holy Ghost, whom the Father will send in my name, He shall teach you all things, and bring all things to your remembrance whatsoever I have said unto you." (Jno. 14:26.) "He shall receive of mine, and show it unto you." (Jno. 16:14.) In these Scriptures the inspiration of the Spirit promised to the disciples is to enable them to *remember* what Jesus had said to them. No new revelations were promised them. But in the performance of their duties in making the gospel known, whether orally or by written statements, they should have the power and guidance of the Spirit to insure to them a correct memory of what He had taught them, thus guarding them against all error.

This work of the Spirit is an inspiration, and a sure protection against mistakes in the propagation of the gospel of salvation to man, and leads His subject "into all (sacred) truth."

Just here arises the question as the *nature* of the Inspiration thus imparted. Was it verbal, or what is known as "*plenary*"? or was it only an impartation of the thought or truth which left the writer to express it in his own language? On this question it is known that there is a difference of opinion among Biblical students and exegetes—some holding one, and some the other view. No doubt both parties are honest in their convictions. But I can not see why such a difference should exist, nor why there should be so much *discussion* of the question, for, as I understand the parties to this discussion, all agree that the Spirit guided the willing and obedient minds of those whom He inspired into *the truth*, whether done by a dictation of the very words, or by dictating the facts or doctrine only, leaving the scribe to clothe it in his own language.

But a question arises as to whether it is possible for a man to think—to have a thought—except as he clothes it in what we call language. Can man think without some symbol or language embodying his thought? To my mind it is utterly impossible. Thought must have some sensible form in which to reside. A thought without a vehicle of thought is to me unthinkable. This vehicle may represent articulate sounds, or mere vocals; it may be lingual or manual, pictorial or hieroglyphical, objective or subjective, but, whatever it may be, it serves the purpose of language. This being true, it is impossible to impart an idea or a thought to the human mind except through the medium of language, or that which supplies its place and is its equivalent.

As to the metaphysical questions of mental operations and their laws, I do not propose to discuss them here. I treat this question simply as one of fact. And, as a fact, man can no more think without a vehicle of thought than he can think of color without thinking of a colored object. Now let the reader make experiment and see whether he can think of color in the abstract, i. e., without a colored object. I am sure that the experiment will prove that a thought without something corresponding to what we mean by *language*, or a conception of color without a colored object is an impossibility.

The same law applies to our concepts of moral qualities. These are all unthinkable apart from a subject, as goodness, wisdom, etc. We can not think of them in the abstract.

The conclusion from this fact, then, is, that a divine inspiration imparted to man necessitates a plenary or verbal inspiration. *Necessarily*, according to the teachings of the Bible itself, and to this law of mental operations this is a Book the very words of which are dictated by the Holy Spirit. But this is so done that the individuality of the several scribes is preserved throughout.

In general terms then

DIVINE INSPIRATION

is such an impartation of the Holy Spirit's influences to man as teaches him the will of God, and prompts him to willing and loving obedience to that will, guiding him in the ways of truth and holiness. It is, as the word indicates, an in-breathing of the Holy Spirit into the soul of man, and to that extent imparting to it the divine nature.

According to this view, such impartation has not been confined to any age of the race of man. That fullness of the inspiration which may be called *miraculous* may have passed away with the Apostles, but the holy impulses imparted to man by the Spirit of God to-day may be properly called inspirations. There may be, and doubtless are various degrees of the Holy Spirit's influences imparted to different persons, and to the same persons at different times. But every holy purpose, every holy desire, every earnest prayer, every sacred joy and every truly righteous act is a result of the in-breathing of the Holy Spirit. *They are not of earth.* "Without me ye can do nothing"

[good]. (John 15:5.) "Likewise, the Spirit helpeth our infirmities; for we know not what we should pray for as we ought." (Rom. 8:26.)

Our loving Saviour has promised the abiding presence and aid of the Spirit to all His disciples to the end of time. Nor do I regard these operations of His Spirit as mere illuminations. Every act of true Christian obedience is the result of Spiritual influence upon man's heart—an impelling, constraining power. But He teaches no new doctrines—makes no new revelations. He enlightens men through the Word, which He has already given and moves them to obedience to that Word. He begets in men a hatred of sin and a love of holiness.

CHAPTER II.

MANY PORTIONS OF THE BIBLE NOT INSPIRED.

BEFORE entering upon the line of proof and argument which I propose to pursue in the discussion of this subject, in order to prevent confusion, I think it well to consider some preliminary matters. Of course such matters are familiar to those who have had the time and facilities for studying them. But as I write for the benefit of the masses who have not had such opportunities for investigation as well as for others who have, I think it well to notice the topic of this chapter somewhat in detail, especially as it has furnished occasions to certain classes of scoffers to disturb the spiritual peace of earnest believers. Hence the matters referred to assume an importance which would not otherwise attach to them. It is a recognized principle, that whatever essentially affects a man's *religious* life is important.

When we say that the Bible was written by men inspired of God, it is not meant that the entire contents—all its statements—are the dictations of the Holy Spirit. No one has ever claimed this. Very many passages are *quotations* from wicked men, while others record the language of demons, and others still the language of the arch-fiend himself. This will evidently occur to even a casual reader of the Book. I will give a few out of the many examples of this character, taking some from the Old Testament and some from the New.

"And Pharaoh said: Who is the Lord that I should obey his voice to let Israel go? I know not the Lord, neither will I let Israel go." (Ex. 5:2.) Of course we know that this entire passage, except the first three words, is not only uninspired of God, but it is the language of a wicked tyrant who, as he said, "knew nothing" of the God of Israel, who is the Author of the Book.

Again: "And he (Sanballat) spake before his brethren and the army of Samaria and said: What do these feeble Jews? Will they fortify themselves? Will they sacrifice? Will they make an end in a day? Will they revive the stones out of the heaps of rubbish which are burned? Now Tobiah the Ammonite was by him, and he said: Even that which they build, if a fox go up, he shall even break down their stone wall." (Neh. 4:2,3.) The language of Sanballat and Tobiah, here inserted by the historian, so far from being inspired by the Holy Spirit, is the language of scorn and derision against the people of God, and, hence, against God Himself.

"Then Jezebel sent a messenger unto Elijah, saying, So let the Gods do to me, and more also, if I make not thy life as one of them [the prophets of Baal whom Elijah had slain] by to-morrow about this time." (I Ki. 19:2.) This is the message which Jezebel, that wicked and idolatrous queen, wife of the wicked king of Israel, Ahab, sent to Elijah when she learned of the slaughter of her priests, the priests of Baal, after that wonderful display of divine interposition on mount Carmel, when fire came down from heaven and consumed the sacrifice which Elijah, His true prophet, had placed upon the altar—in which incident there is a fearful display of the severity of divine justice against false teachers who lead the people astray with false doctrines and lying wonders; and a wonderful manifestation of divine power and mercy in the vindication of His true and obedient servants.

Of course a great many passages of a similar character might be quoted from the Old Testament Scriptures. But I forbear; nor would I have *quoted* these, but that I suppose the average reader would hardly pause to examine them simply from a reference to them.

Passing for the present from the Old we will note a few instances of such records of uninspired matter found in the

NEW TESTAMENT.

Without quoting the many charges preferred against Jesus and His doctrines, by ungodly Scribes and Pharisees, during His active ministry, all of which He turned against themselves, and thereby vindicated His claim to be the Son of God, suppose we turn to the accounts given by the Evangelists of His arrest, trial, condemnation and crucifixion, and strike therefrom all that is reported to have been said by ungodly men, His murderers, who were parties to the proceedings that culminated in His death, what real intelligence could we have of the various stages in the enactment of that awful tragedy? In what way could the condemnation and crucifixion of Jesus have been justified from a civil or legal point of view without a knowledge of the influence which the Jews exerted upon the Roman governor, Pilate? and how could we know the nature and the extent of that influence without a knowledge of what they said—the charges they preferred against Him, false though they were, and the arguments they used, however flimsy, to compass their end—the death of Jesus?

A great many instances similar to these here given might be cited from both Testaments, but these are sufficient to indicate what we mean when we say that there are many *uninspired* passages in the Bible, i. e., passages not dictated by the Spirit of God, and therefore, in that sense are not inspired.

But while their utterance was not by the dictation of the Spirit of God, their insertion into the Bible was—they are there by divine guidance and authority. Holy men of old were prompted by the Spirit of God to insert just enough of these uninspired and wicked utterances of men and devils to serve the purposes of infinite Love and Wisdom in making known

His will to the children of men. Without such insertions the narrative would often be incomplete, and hence unintelligible. As an illustration: The inspired prayer of Nehemiah, which, in the Record, immediately follows the language of Sanballat and Tobiah quoted above, would be pointless and unintelligible without a knowledge of the immediate antecedent cause, the sarcastic utterances and threatening attitude of these enemies. And the same may be said concerning the statements and the facts connected with the defiant language of Pharaoh concerning the divine commands to let the children of Israel go. It requires a knowledge of his rejection of the divine authority to enable us to see the justice of the severity of the punishments inflicted upon him and his kingdom as recorded in the Book of "Exodus." Nor could the flight of Elijah from the scenes of his former triumphs and his concealment in the wilderness with their related facts be accounted for without a knowledge of the threat that Jezebel had made that she would have him slain.

These instances are given simply as indicative of the necessity for the insertion of much uninspired language to the completeness of the

Record and to a proper understanding of the facts stated. In other words: They are necessary to connected narrative, and to the development of the causes of subsequent events and their relation to antecedent facts. And, besides this, they serve to illustrate the justice and mercy exercised by the divine Ruler in His government of the race and "Thus vindicate the ways of God to men."

Hence, to reject the doctrine of the inspiration and consequent authority of the Bible because of the presence of such passages as are confessedly uninspired is to defy reason and reject the plainest dictates of propriety and common sense, and to stultify the universal practice of the best writers, sacred and profane, ancient and modern.

Instead of affording an argument against the inspiration and consequent trustworthiness of the Bible, properly considered, they confirm both in a variety of ways, a few of which are the following: (1) It touches profane history in simple allusions but with a directness and fearlessness of contradiction which is striking and which indicates conscious truthfulness, giving the names and nationalities of the speakers and the actors, whose language is quoted and whose actions are recorded. This fact combined with the simplicity of their style and evident consciousness of veracity of their record on the part of the writers rationally *compel belief.* (2) By the insertion of these uninspired utterances many historical facts are accounted for which would otherwise be unaccountable. How could we account for the peaceful returns of the Jews from their captivity in Babylon to their own Canaan without a knowledge of the "Decrees" issued by Cyrus, and Darius, and Darius Hystaspes with all their related facts as recorded by Ezra and Nehemiah? Without these documents being given, we should have ground for serious doubt as to the truthfulness of the Record; but with these "Decrees" before us all is clear.

Thus we might continue to specify cases *ad lib.* which go to show the necessity there was for the insertion of the uninspired matter into the divine Book, that the truth might appear, and that "*Holy* men of old" were moved by the Holy Spirit to incorporate these sayings of wicked men and of devils into the Book of divine Inspiration. But these instances are sufficient.

Before passing from the consideration of uninspired sayings incorporated with the inspired portions of the Bible, I think it well to notice the question whether it is admissible for the preacher to use such uninspired portions as texts or bases of sermons. It is known that some, perhaps a majority, of our best and wisest writers on the subject object to such use being made of them. But to my mind the objection rests on insufficient ground. That is, *they are no parts of the Inspired Word of God.* I offer the following suggestions: Though known to be uninspired, they have been put into the volume of Inspiration under the guidance of the Holy Spirit, as claimed above, and as admitted by all who claim or admit the Bible to be the Word of God. And while this fact may not be recognized as sufficient proof that such passages may be used as texts for sermons, it is, at least, *presumptive* evidence that they may be so used. But Paul's language to Timothy (2 Tim. 3:16, 17) seems to put the question to rest in the affirmative: "All Scripture is given by inspiration of God, and is profitable," etc. Or, if we accept the Canterbury revision, "All Scripture given," etc., the affirmative is still more strongly sustained. In either case, the volume of inspiration as a whole is referred to, and the affirmative is sustained.

Besides, is it not true that our Saviour, on several occasions, used the language of some of His bitterest enemies as texts for short sermons? There are two such sermons recorded in the 12th chapter of Matthew's gospel, one beginning with the 24th verse, and ending with the 37th; the other beginning with the 39th verse and ending with the 45th. The first is based on the charge of the Pharisees, that he cast out devils through Beelzebub, the prince of the devils. The second was based upon the language of the Scribes and Pharisees when they said to Him, "Master, we would see a sign from thee." No doubt the "Master" preached much longer sermons from these texts than have been reported by Matthew, or Mark, or Luke, all of whom report these sermons more or less fully. And there are many other similar instances which will recur to the mind of the reader very readily, at least, if at all familiar with the gospels.

On the day of Pentecost when under the influence of the miraculous effusion of the Holy Spirit, "The disciples began to speak with other tongues, as the Spirit gave them utterance," and the multitude were astonished at what they saw and heard, some of them said: "These men are full of new wine." Then Peter arose, and if he did not take the charge of intoxication as a text, he certainly used it as the occasion for the sermon he preached on that day—that memorable sermon on that memorable day, for he began by saying: "These are not drunk as ye suppose."

For these and other reasons which I need not now give, with all due respect for the opinions of others, and with the highest esteem for their scholarship and judgment, in matters pertaining to Biblical interpretation and homiletical propriety, I must demur to the idea of the inadmissibility of such Scriptures as proper topics or texts for pulpit or sermonic discussion. Take, for example: "Almost thou persuadest me to be a Christian"; "Paul, thou art beside thyself, much learning doth make thee mad," etc., etc.

CHAPTER III.

MAN'S TEMPTATION AND FALL. THE TEMPTER.

THUS far we have considered in a general way the *fact* and the *nature* of inspiration and some reasons for the insertion of uninspired matter or language in the volume of divine Inspiration, and, incidentally, the use that the preacher may make of these uninspired portions as texts or bases for pulpit ministrations. Nor do I call to mind a single instance of the insertion of uninspired language the insertion of which is not necessary to a proper comprehension of the incidents or the doctrines with the narration or statement of which it stands connected. Should any claim that such instances exist, it will rest with such claimant to point them out.

There is in the Bible a brief account of an occurrence which lies at the base of human history, and which demands more than a passing notice. I refer to the source or origin of all our woe in this life and the life to come; and at the risk of being considered tedious, I propose to notice it somewhat in detail. Of course, I refer to the temptation and fall of man from his original state of innocence, and which is described as having been accomplished by the being called "the devil" in the form of a "serpent."

In this account of that sad event the very words employed by the serpent in the temptation he presented to Eve are recorded and are absolutely essential to a complete understanding of the transaction with all its related facts and doctrines. Omit the tempter's language as it is recorded in the first five verses of Gen., III chap., and the history is so mutilated as to become unintelligible. That many perplexing questions arise in regard to the scenes and facts stated in the record, is freely admitted. But that can not discredit the narrative given. We are brought into daily contact—face to face, as it were—with thousands of facts as mysterious to us as this is. And, yet, with all this mystery, this is the most *rational* account of man's sad and sinful condition of any yet presented, or invented. No other theory adequately accounts for man's *existence*, or for his *condition* in life.

Whether the facts here recorded concerning the fall of man and the sentences pronounced upon him and the serpent were, *primarily* matters of supernatural *revelation* to the writer of Genesis as we now have it, or only a result of divine *inspiration*, may admit of a doubt. It is possible that Adam was inspired of God to make a record of the temptation and fall from his personal knowledge of the facts.

That the "serpent" which was made the agent in the temptation through Satanic influence, was a very different animal from what it has been since, is clear from the description here given of it. "Now the serpent was more subtle (*shrewd, cunning*,) than any beast of the field which the Lord God had made." (1.) Then, it belonged, not to the *genus* of "creeping things" here classed together, but to the *beasts* of the field" or wild beasts. (2.) It constituted a *species* of this *genus*. The comparison, then is that of the *serpent species*, with *all the other species* of the same *genus*. In this comparison, it is called the shrewdest, the most cunning of them all, the *anthropomorphic apes not excepted*. By the Biblical nomenclature, used in this connection, terrestrial animals, man excepted, were divided into three *genera*, viz.: "Cattle, 'creeping things' and beasts of the field," or wild beasts. Under this classification the serpent, *as it now is*, would belong to the class, creepers. But the writer of Genesis calls it a "beast of the field," thereby placing it in the third class of his classification, otherwise his comparison is bewildering in the extreme.

Again: The serpent that was used as the agent in the betrayal of the woman into sin *spake* to her in articulate language, nay, more, in *human* speech, and through the satanic influence which controlled him (*or* it) "beguiled" her into a violation of her Maker's command.

That the beast, here called "Serpent," was at that time the most highly organized and endowed of all terrestrial animals, *man only excepted*, to my mind, does not admit of a doubt. One of the results of the *divine curse* put upon it was that it should henceforth "go upon its belly." If this had been its previous manner of locomotion, there would have been no punishment in it, and yet it is stated as part of the punishment inflicted for allowing himself made the agent of man's sin and consequent fall.

Moreover: The language of Jehovah in pronouncing his sentence seems to indicate that the serpent possessed sufficient *moral* nature, and, hence, moral responsibility to make it a fit subject for punishment on moral grounds. "Because thou hast done this, thou art cursed above all cattle and above every beast of the field." This is what the "Lord God said to the serpent." This language clearly implies that the serpent had consciously and willingly lent himself to the perpetration of a crime against God, and that he had sinned against man, and "beguiled" him to his ruin is implied in the fact that God "*Put enmity* between him and the woman," etc. He must, therefore, have possessed a *moral nature* though it may have been and doubtless was of a very low type, as the punishment inflicted was *purely corporeal.*

With this transformation, involved in the curse pronounced upon it, the type of the original serpent ended. Possibly, this is the "Missing Link," which a certain class of scientists have so long and laboriously sought for in vain. With the transformation named above the primordial *serpent-species* ceased and was succeeded by or changed into the form and nature of the serpent of succeeding ages. One fact in favor of the idea of its being the "Missing Link" is, that it touches the human age, and that is one of the conditions required by said scientists. The original of the species beginning and ending with the first individual of that form of the species could not leave a fossil of its primal form.

I am aware of the fact that this hypothesis does not meet the requirements of Mr. Darwin's theory of Evolution, but it may *indicate* the fallacy of his theory and help his followers to find that "*missing link*."

In this account of man's fall from his primitive purity and happiness we have the only satisfactory solution of his present sad condition. But it is worthy of remark, that every reference to man's sinful and unhappy condition in the Bible, however remote the reference may be, or however incidental, points back to the sad scenes of Eden, as described in the 3d. chapter of Genesis, as the solution of the question of this sad state. The devil told Eve a long time ago that God had lied, and Huxley, Haeckel, *et id omne genus*, is telling the same thing now.

Accepting the condition of things as described

in the record, the process of the temptation as presented is natural and consistent with itself and that condition. The tempter approaches the *woman* in the person of that type of animal nearest the human, speaks to her in human language, manifests the intensest interest in and desire for the happiness and welfare of herself and husband. By these means, having gained her attention and interest in what he is saying, the way is open for the consummation of his diabolical purpose. I suppose he took of the forbidden fruit and ate it in her presence, to convince her it was harmless. "And when the woman *saw* that the tree was good for food she took of the fruit thereof and did eat, and gave also unto her husband with her, and he did eat."

> "Earth felt the wound and nature from her seat,
> Sighing through all her works, gave signs of
> Woe, that all was lost."

Thus was man introduced to the arch enemy of God, and man, through whose lying flattery Paradise was lost and man driven forth to toil, and want, and pain, and disappointment, and sorrow, and death, and made the victim of the thousands of ills which affect him in this life, and, except as redeemed and saved by the blood of Christ Jesus—"the Seed of the woman,"—the inheritor of everlasting woe in the world to come—the eternal ages:

> "The fruit
> Of that forbidden tree, whose mortal taste
> Brought *death into the world*, and ALL OUR WOE."

The scenes here described transpired thousands of years ago, and yet this same enemy plies the same arts, pursues the same plan, practices the same wiles, and still succeeds in beguiling the children of the woman to their ruin by his devices. This is, in brief, the *Biblical* account of the introduction of sin into the world. It is short, simple, direct, and related with an air of truth, and bears the impress of the divine Author.

It is to be observed, too, that the traits or elements of character of the arch deceiver presented in this narrative are *persistently* preserved throughout the entire volume of Inspiration. Wherever referred to, whether by Patriarch, Lawgiver, Poet or Prophet; or by our Lord or his apostles the elements of his character as developed in this history of the temptation are constant quantities. He is the same deceiver, liar, tempter, enemy of God and of all righteousness, the destroyer of the peace and happiness of mankind. He is the same insidious, malevolent, active and dangerous being whether called "devil," or "satan," or "apolyon," or "dragon," or "serpent," or "the prince of the power of the air," or "the father of lies." Everywhere in the Bible he has individuality and the elements of personality. And while there is no formal description given of his *origin* or of his *manner* of being there is no mistaking the *elements* of his being nor his power over men. He is nowhere in the Bible represented as a myth or a mere principle of evil inherent in mundane existences, or in matter. His very nature is moral corruption—the aggregation of all evil. Evil, and only evil, and always evil.

Several questions are sometimes asked as a sort of parry to appeals made to serve God: "Where did the devil come from?" "Why did God allow him to tempt man?" "Where did sin originate?" etc.

We may not be able to answer such questions. But that sin is in the world is clearly enough to be seen. That all men are sinners is clear. That sin will be punished is testified by the race. The practical question is: What will I, you, do about it? That this uniformity of description of the satanic nature and influence should be preserved throughout the writings constituting our Bible without divine guidance is hardly to be supposed possible; and especially does the improbability, at least, of such a fact appear when we remember that the writers of the Bible lived and wrote amid very diverse environments, possessed various degrees of natural and of acquired abilities, and that the time of their composition embraced a period of at least 1500 years—from the death of Moses to that of John—(and this is affirmed the "Higher Criticism," to the contrary notwithstanding).

But as it respects the consistency and harmony observable throughout our sacred Oracles in the work attributed to the devil, they certainly show that the writers whatever may have been their individual peculiarites of mental constitution, or of their environments, must have been guided by the same Spirit. This identity of description or of representation is not found among pagan writers in their descriptions of their demons. Whence this difference between the two classes of writers? I think it clear that it arises from the fact that one class was guided by the Spirit of God, the other was not.

CHAPTER IV.

DEITY.

BY the universal consent of the race, there is a supreme POWER, who is the Creator and Ruler of the universe, though unseen by man. All the nations of the earth recognize the existence of such a Power or Being. It is true that there are and have been individual exceptions to the rule, men who deny the existence of a Supreme Ruler. "The *fool* hath said in his heart there is no God." There are men who, though the creatures of God and the subjects of His constant care, and the recipients of His unfailing mercies, eliminate Him from the universe He has created and sustains. "Professing themselves to be wise they are become fools." "The carnal mind is emnity against God" solves the question of the denial of His existence and sovereignty. It is "Because men do not like to retain God in their thoughts" nor submit to His authority that they fail to see Him in His works and spurn His Word.

The Bible reveals God to man—the one only living and true God, besides whom there is no God. And among the writers of all these Books constituting our Bible, with all their diversified talents, tastes and conditions of life, there are no discrepancies nor variations in representations in regard to Him. What He is in Genesis He is throughout the entire Record, without a shadow of inconsistency or variation. Unlike the Gods of the heathen nations, He is ONE, and is neither a myth, nor chance, nor blind fate, nor a deified human hero, nor an abstraction. In every reference to Him, He is the same GOD unchanged and unchangeable.

It is very true, that the nature of His being and His attributes are not fully manifested *ab initio.* On the contrary, His divine character, the purposes of His divine government, and the plan and means for the accomplishment of these purposes are harmoniously unfolded. Happy is he who comprehends and conforms to this plan.

This gradual development of the moral economy of the divine government is in harmony with the gradual developments observable in the material world. Some one has said:

Natura saltem non noscit. This simply means that God has proceeded, and still proceeds by regular *gradations* to accomplish His purposes in the natural world. This law of development or evolution along given lines is everywhere manifest both in the material and immaterial realms of nature. It would, therefore, appear very strange indeed, if He had made an exception to this otherwise universal law of His own appointment and observance, in His moral realm, and had made a full and complete revelation of Himself, His plan of moral government over the world and the consummation of all His purposes from the beginning. Had He thus done it would have given strong grounds for rational doubt whether the God of nature is the God of the Bible, so diverse would the methods of procedure have been.

But however gradual or slow the development of the nature of His being and of His attributes; and the nature of His government over and gracious purposes toward man have been and still are, there are entire harmony and uniformity in the delineations given of them all in His Word—The Bible. There is no contradiction, nor even contrariety, except in forms of expression, in the descriptions given. Every where He is the same God, revealing Himself to man more and more through various institutions and communications, "At sundry times and in divers manners," until, "In thé fulness of time" He put on human flesh and "dwelt among us," as the Son, "full of grace and truth," "The brightness of the Father's glory, and the express image of His person" and "In whom dwelleth all the fulness of the God-head (Deity) bodily." Every reference to Him or to His nature in the entire Bible is harmonious with each other, the only possible difference being that one may be more or less elaborate than another. The God of the Bible never contradicts Himself. The God of Adam is the God of Enoch, and of Abraham and the Patriarchs, and of Moses and of all the Prophets, and of the Apostles—the God of heaven and of earth—the everlasting and unchangeable God—"the living and the true God," "Besides whom there is no God."

The same God who said to Adam: "Of the tree of the knowledge of good and evil, thou shalt not eat of it: for in the day thou eatest thereof thou shalt surely die" (Heb. dying, thou shalt die) said through John on the isle of Patmos: "The Spirit and the bride say, Come; and let him that heareth say, Come; and whosoever will, let him take the water of life freely." "To him that overcometh, I will give to eat of the tree of life which is in the midst of the Paradise of God." And this last message of God to man is but the *consummation* of His purpose as expressed in the garden of Eden: I will put enmity between thee (the serpent) and the woman, and between thy seed and her seed: it shall bruise thy head, and thou shalt bruise his heel."

Thus through a long series of developments, the obscure promise of Eden develops into the ineffable glories of Patmos.

The supreme gods of the most enlightened heathen nations of antiquity were fickle, capricious, vengeful, lewd, and themselves subject to inexorable Fate. "So the Fates have decreed" was the end of controversy in the councils of their gods. These *decrees* were unalterable however much their supreme god, *Jupiter* or *Zeus* might wish it otherwise.

In the incidental delineations of the being and nature of the God of the Bible, there is a dignity and stateliness of portraiture compared with which the rhapsodies of a Homer or a Virgil dwindle into the merest puerilities, though the products of lofty poetic genius.

Is it possible to account for the exalted tone of style, the grandeur of sentiment, the sublimity of conception, and the perfect harmony in the description of the God of the Bible, among so many writers of such diverse endowments, living in such widely separated ages and amidst such various environments as did the original writers of the Bible, except upon the supposition that they were guided by the same Spirit? and, that that Spirit was the Holy Spirit of God? Upon any other supposition the composition of the Bible is the most stupendous miracle imaginable. All the miracles it records would dwindle into insignificance in comparison with it.

The writers of our Bible never entered upon an argument to prove by logical processes that God exists. Their proofs are facts, not theories nor arguments. Neither did they *assume* that there is a God, as we sometimes hear. If there was any assumption in the matter, it was that man, the race, recognized the existence of

God, as Creator and Ruler of the universe He had created. Nor do we anywhere in the Bible find any detailed or connected portraiture or description of His nature and attributes. These writers *knew* that God existed. As well might we say that a man having the full possession of all his physical organs of sense in healthy exercise assumes the existence of the *sun*, or any of the material things with which he comes into daily contact. It is common for us to assume that *those whom we address* know that there is a sun and a world of matter round about them. This is according to facts.

The Sacred writers knew that God exists, for He made Himself known to them. This He did in various ways. The most usual manner seems to have been by *oral* communications. "God who at sundry times and in divers manners spake unto the fathers by the prophets, etc." He spake to Adam both before and after the fall. He spake to Cain after he had become a fratricide. He spake to Noah and to Abraham, to Isaac, and to Jacob; to Moses and Samuel, and to a long line of prophets under the Old Dispensation. He talked to these holy men as man talks to man. If asked how we know He thus spake to them, we reply: (1) *They say He did*, and their testimony is uncontradicted by any *competent* witness. (2) This testimony bears every mark of truthfulness. (a) It is given in such a simple and direct manner that it commands, and to an earnest, honest inquirer, compels assent to its truthfulness. The candor and honesty of these writers are shown by the fact that they record their own sins and mistakes, and their consequent reproof and condemnation therefor in the same manner as they do their obedience to God and consequent blessing. This is not the practice of imposters and false witnesses. These writers have "Nothing concealed, nothing extenuated, nor set down aught in malice." Their very style proclaims that they have "plain unvarnished" truths unfolded. Their statements bear upon their faces the stamp of honesty and truthfulness. (b) They have been accepted as true by those who are their lineal descendents, who have preserved and venerated them as holy writings, divinely inspired from the remotest ages of recorded time. The contents of the writings, including the Revelations they have made which were future at the times of their composition, have been such as no mere human sagacity of any age could have conceived. The fulfilment of their prophecies has attested their divine inspiration. In their very terms as well as in their spirit they differ as widely from the frenzied utterances from the celebrated Delphic Oracle as light does from darkness. Now I emphasize this question, why this difference? (d) The writings of the Old Testament were quoted and endorsed by our Lord Jesus Christ and his inspired Apostles as of Divine authority. (e) The history of the descendants of Abraham and the present condition of the Jews afford strong corroborative proof of the truthfulness of both the Old and the New Testament Scriptures, and hence, of their divine origin and authority.

These writings alone solve the thousands of enigmas of not only Jewish but of human history.

It is not in the line of my purpose to discuss at present these several points, nor even to adduce passages or facts in illustration of them. But such is their aggregate force and value, in my estimation, that when one of these holy (not perfect) men says that the "Lord said unto Moses, (or Noah, etc.) thus and so," I am constrained to believe him—*rationally*, I can not refuse to believe. (3) The holiest and some of the wisest men of whom history gives us any knowledge received this Word as divine Truth, and ascribed whatever of merit they possessed to its mysterious influence. With Paul they would say: "By the grace of God, I am what I am." To this rule there is no exception. When Jesus prayed: "Sanctify them (his disciples) through thy truth, thy Word is truth," he evidently referred to the Old Testament Scriptures, as well as to His own sublime teachings, as God's truth; for He said: "I have given them thy Word," and the prayer and declaration were in unison with the facts of human history and experience. The sanctification of the human heart is by the Holy Spirit through the Word of God only. There are no other means, there is no other power by and through which this great and needed change can be accomplished but the Truth of God. No other system of ethics or of religion possesses such sanctifying power. The wisdom of the world has *signally failed* to meet the demands of the human soul, the wants of the race in regard to their most important interests, and these are the interests with which this Book deals and for which, according to the testimony of millions of the purest of the race, of both the living and the dead, this Book presents ample provisions.

With all these proofs before us how can we entertain a rational doubt that the facts and doctrines made known to man in the Bible have been communicated to him by his Maker for his instruction, and comfort, and guidance amid the perplexities, and trials, and sorrows of this life? And it is to be borne in mind that this is not the testimony of *some*, but of *all* the myriads of witnesses who have been made partakers of an experimental knowledge of the grace revealed and proffered to men in these sacred pages. They all recognize the fact that Jehovah has spoken to those men whom He has chosen and sent as His messengers to the race, and as the Author of the messages they have delivered, whether they were delivered to them by divine *oral* instruction or simply by their conscious experience of the impulses of the Holy Spirit upon their hearts.

That the various writers of these sixty-six

books which constitute our Bible, writing as they did, under such diverse conditions, amid such diverse environments, with such varieties of natural and acquired abilities and tastes,—should thus uniformly present the same conceptions of Deity is inconceivable except upon the supposition that Jehovah revealed a knowledge of Himself and of His will to them in some supernatural manner.

CHAPTER V.

DIVINE ATTRIBUTES.

THE truth presented in the preceding chapter is more clearly shown and more emphatically confirmed by the entire harmony observable among the writers of the Bible in their more specific references to what are known among Theological writers as the "*divine attributes.*"

These attributes constitute the elements of His *being*, and are essential to the idea of Deity. This is equivalent to saying that, deprived of these "attributes" He would cease to be God. That He possesses these attributes to a degree and in a manner beyond our comprehension is, from the very nature of the case, unquestionably true. And that He possesses other attributes, perfectly harmonious with these, which have not been revealed to us, and of the nature of which we can have no conception, is in a high degree probable. But, even if that be so, He has made such a revelation of Himself to man in His Word, as He saw fit to make; neither are we prepared to say that any additional revelations would have been, or would now be profitable to man.

Deity has seen fit graciously to make Himself known to us as self-existent, eternal, all-wise, all-powerful; as infinite in justice, mercy, truth, love and holiness; as the Creator and Ruler of all things, whether in heaven above or in earth beneath; and as the Author of human redemption and salvation through Christ Jesus.

It is not my purpose to discuss these attributes now. I only wish to call attention to the fact, that the Sacred Record everywhere *recognizes these* as the characteristics of Jehovah—God. There are no discrepancies, no contradictions, no variations in this regard throughout the entire volume of Inspiration. Just as these attributes are developed in the first three chapters of Genesis (as far as that development goes) so they are preserved throughout the entire Record, whenever the writers have occasion to refer to them, however remote the reference may be. If it be objected that some of these attributes are incompatible with each other, or contradictory of each other, as for example to say, that one and the same Being is at the same time *infinitely just* and, infinitely merciful is to state an impossible condition, the one being inconsistent with the other, I reply: *That* is not the question under present consideration. The question at present regards simply the entire *harmony of the writers of the Bible in ascribing these attributes to the Being we call God.* And I insist that the unanimity with which these writers ascribe these elements of His nature and being to Him is utterly unaccountable upon any other theory than that *one Spirit* guided them all in their conceptions and descriptions of Deity.

In illustration of this point let us compare a few statements made by different writers, at very different ages, and, consequently, under very different conditions of the human race: Look at the account given of the transactions in the garden of Eden both before and after the fall of man, as recorded in the first few chapters of Genesis. In this portion of the divine Word several of the attributes of Deity are developed in such a manner as to demand our closest attention.

God is declared to be the Creator of "The

heavens and the earth" in the beginning "of their existence." (The Hebrew term for "God" employed here is *Elohim.*) This is equivalent to saying that He has all power—is omnipotent. (Gen. 1:1.) Of course this was a matter of pure revelation to the human scribe, whoever he might have been. In the light of modern science, there can be but little, if any room for doubt that the creation here described antedated the creation of man by many millions of years. Nor is this view at all in conflict with the Sacred narrative, when properly understood. But whenever and however this creative energy may have been exerted, God was the Creator.

This is the *initial* presentation of the idea of God (Elohim) to the human race, and it is that of omnipotent creative power. If now we turn to "Revelation," (21:5) we read: "And He (God) that sat upon the throne, said, Behold I make all things new." That the Book of "Revelation" was written at least 1500 years after the Book of Genesis was written in the form in which we now have it, and under widely different conditions of the race civilly, intellectually and religiously, does not admit of a rational doubt. And yet this almightiness which is ascribed to God in the first verse of Genesis is also ascribed to Him here in the latest Book of the Bible. And more striking still are the following passages found in "Revelation," "Holy, holy, holy, Lord God Almighty, which was, and is, and is to come . . . . Thou art worthy, O Lord, to receive glory and honor and power: for thou hast created all things, and for thy pleasure they are and were created." (Rev. 4:8–11.) In these passages the same creative power, involving the idea of Omnipotence, is ascribed to God that is declared of Him in Genesis, with the additional attribute of holiness, and a statement of the reason or object of creation, viz., the divine pleasure. And yet the *style* of John in the "Revelation" is as different from that employed by the writer of Genesis as were the conditions under which they wrote.

And thus it is through all the intervening Books. Whenever the writers have occasion to refer to the matter, however remotely, God, whether simply God, (*Elohim*) or (*Yehovah Elohim*) Lord God of the Old Testament; or God, (*Theos*) or (*Kurios ho Theos*) of the New Testament He is invariably recognized as the

Omnipotent one. Whatever may be our conception of the meaning of these terms employed by the sacred writers to express the nature of this self-existent Creator, there can not be any rational doubt that they used them in identically the *same* sense. Just the Being whom the penman of Genesis calls "Elohim," John in the Revelation calls "Theos." Throughout the entire Bible He is presented to us as the *same* God, infinite and perfect in all the attributes of His being.

Without stopping to discuss them, I will note the following additional facts as illustrative of the attributes, and hence of the nature and prerogatives of God, as harmoniously portrayed by these writers, however varied their environments and their phraseology.

In Gen. 2, the Lord God asserts His sovereignty over man, fixing his abode, placing him in it, and giving him authoritative directions as to what he *might* do, and what he *must not do*, with an announcement of the penalty which would be inflicted upon him in case of disobedience. In all this His claim to govern man is clearly implied. This same authority is claimed throughout these sacred Oracles, without the least variation or abatement and in unmistakable terms. In no instance is He represented as relaxing this claim or in any sense abating His "right to reign" absolutely over the works of His hand. He is "King of kings and Lord of lords." In this regard all the writers of the Bible from Moses to John are as *one*. This is a constant quantity amidst all the variations of human modes of thought and all the vicissitudes of mundane affairs. From the first to the last utterances of these writers the rule is: *Obey God and live*, or *disobey Him and die.* According to the undeviating tenor of His Word, Jehovah demands of all men everywhere, at all times and under all conditions, entire submission to His will and implicit obedience to His laws; and all this not simply because he has a right to such submission, but also because by such obedience man's happiness and best interests are conserved—or in other words: "All His ways are pleasantness and all His paths are peace" to man. He is ever present everywhere "beholding the evil and the good" and will in the end bring every work into judgment. None can evade His power, none escape His hands. "His kingdom ruleth over all" and "All that

He does is done in righteousness and in truth," for "He is just and righteous in all His ways."

As far as possible, the writers sink themselves out of sight, and present only their themes. In fact many of these writings are anonymous. But whether we have the names of the writers or not, the uniformity of their descriptions of the being, nature and attributes of God are marvelous, if not utterly inexplicable, upon any other hypothesis than that of having been dictated by the same Spirit, and that Spirit was none other than the Spirit of the God of infinite wisdom and truth.

CHAPTER VI.

JUSTICE AND MERCY.

ACCORDING to Biblical representation, Justice and Mercy are attributes of Deity. By those who deny or question the divine inspiration and authority of our Scriptures, it is claimed that these attributes are incompatible with each other and, therefore, mutually destructive and are thus fatal to the idea of supernatural inspiration.

It is not my purpose to undertake now to show their harmony and entire compatibility with each other. That task would devolve upon the expositor. My only purpose at present is to call attention to the wonderful harmony which exists among the sacred writers respecting both the existence and constant exercise of these attributes in the administration of the divine government over the world of intelligent moral creatures, and I take again for illustration examples from the first and last of the sixty-six Books of this volume. We learn from the first few chapters of Genesis that God created man in "His own image and likeness" and provided for his happiness by placing him amid environments just suited to his nature and bestowing a suitable companion to cheer his life and to share his joys. In this habitation called the "Garden of Eden" He had collected everything that could minister to their wants, promote their happiness and contribute to their welfare. He gave them full and free use of all the products of the garden *except the fruit of one tree.* But of the fruit of that tree He positively forbade their eating, and told them what would be the result of disobedience. In this grant there is abundant evidence of the goodness of their Creator in thus providing for the happiness of these, His intelligent and moral creatures, but, at the same time there is a clear expression of His authority over them and of their *obligation* to *obey such authority.* These are clearly set forth in the narrative given us of these transactions. I do not assume that Adam and Eve comprehended *all* that was involved in the language of their Creator and Sovereign, but they certainly understood both the privilege granted and, also, the prohibition enjoined: "Of every tree of the garden thou mayest freely eat; but of the tree of the knowledge of good and evil, thou shalt not eat of it; for in the day thou eatest thereof, dying thou shalt die (tr. thou shalt surely die). That they comprehended the full significance of the results that should follow a violation of the prohibition is not probable. But that they understood the meaning of both the privilege and the prohibition is clear from the entire narrative.

The reason here assigned for the prohibition is to be regarded rather as a warning than as a threat. The effect of the fruit forbidden would be death if eaten: "Thou shalt die."

But no warning which was an expression of divine mercy, was disregarded. Adam and Eve, the *primal* pair of the human race, ate of the forbidden fruit and incurred the fearful penalty—*death.* How sad the results have been and will be to their blighted posterity eternity alone can fully reveal. The guilty pair were called to account for their violation of their Sovereign's command, by their own confessions, were adjudged guilty, were driven from the garden which had been their home and were forever debarred the privilege of returning to its hallowed scenes.

> "Oh unexpected stroke, worse than of Death!
> Must I thus leave thee, Paradise? thus leave
> Thee, native soil! these happy walks and shades.
> Fit haunt of Gods?"

Yet, even in pronouncing the sentence of condemnation and banishment, which Justice demanded, there is given an intimation of mercy, a ground of hope. "I will put enmity between thee (the serpent) and the woman, and between thy seed and her seed: He shall bruise thy head, and thou shalt bruise his heel."

This language, though addressed to the serpent, was evidently spoken within the hearing of Adam and Eve. How much of its import they may have comprehended, we are not permitted to know. But it seems clear that in some way they were taught to propitiate the divine favor and trust in His mercy for forgiveness. This is clear, I think, from the fact that their sons, Cain and Abel, "brought offerings to the Lord," and the style of the narrative clearly indicates that these offerings were customary, made at regular intervals of time and that, too, according to the divine requirement, though there is no formal statement of these conditions in the Record. I think this is certain for the following reason: 1. The *rendering* of the Hebrew (Gen. 4:3,) does not, according to high authority, represent the Hebrew correctly. It is more correctly rendered "at the end of days," indicating that there was a specific period at the close of which sacrifices should be offered. 2. It is stated that "Cain brought of the fruit of the ground," but "Abel brought of the firstlings of his flock"—a bloody offering. Cain's offering was rejected. Abel's was *accepted.* Why this difference? I can conceive of but one reason, viz., God had ordered a *bloody* sacrifice as a type of the sacrifice which the seed of the woman would in "the fullness of time" make for the sins of mankind. In that promised sacrifice Abel had faith, Cain did not. (See Heb. 11:4.) Abel did well, though he died for it. Cain did not well. The inference is a necessary one that our first parents had revealed to them more or less clearly the merciful provision of God by which sin would be pardoned and the believing sinner saved.

And yet the guilty pair were driven out of Eden, and made to eat their bread by the sweat of their face. They were subjected to toil, and sorrow, and affliction through their long lives, and "*death*" closed the scene. "In the day thou eatest thereof, dying, thou shalt die."

In this account of the early scenes of human life there is manifest a wonderful intermingling of justice and mercy in the divine dealings with primeval man. And, yet, there is nothing to shock our sense of propriety and fitness in the entire narrative. All is natural and harmonious with our conceptions of justice and mercy in guiding the entire transaction. Nothing seems strange or out of harmony except man's disregard of his Lord's command and consequent sin and ruin by which he has entailed sin and all our woe, both in this world and that which is to come, upon all his posterity. "Wherefore, as by one man sin entered into the world, and *death by sin*; and so death passed upon all men, for that all have sinned." (Rom. 5.12.)

Then, as intimated above, notwithstanding the apparent inconsistency between these divine attributes considered in the abstract, we find them blended in the most harmonious union in the divine proceedings. In fact the divinely harmonious union of these attributes is manifest throughout the Scriptures in the judgments of God towards His fallen creature, man.

"O. the goodness and severity of God."

On the isle of Patmos, the beloved John was, through a divine Revelation, permitted to see the closing scenes of the present order of mundane things, and in almost the closing words of this Revelation, there is presented a wonderfully striking illustration of the harmonious blending of these elements of Jehovah's government over men. I quote a few passages: "But the fearful and unbelieving, and abominable, and murderers and whoremongers, and sorcerers, and idolaters, and all liars shall have their part in the lake which burneth with fire and brimstone: which is the second death." (Rev. 21:8.) "Blessed are they which do His commandments, that they may have right to the tree of life, and may enter in through the gates into the city .... And the Spirit and the bride say: Come. And let him that heareth, say: Come. And let him that is athirst: Come. And whosoever will, let him take the water of life freely." (Rev. 22:14,17.)

In these decrees of the final "Judge of human kind," and in this comprehensive invitation to men to "come" and accept eternal life "*freely*," we find a wonderful harmony between the most rigid execution of justice and the extension of the broadest conceivable mercy to all who will accept it. What more could be asked?

Thus, as in the first act in the wonderfully grand drama of human life, which opened amid the beauties, the fragrance, the purity and the bliss of an unforfeited Paradise, there is found an indiscribable but harmonious blending of the sternest justice and the gentlest mercy: so in the last scene of the last act, when "the heavens shall pass away with a great noise, and the elements shall melt with fervent heat; the earth also and the works therein shall be burned up;" when the "Great white throne and He that sits upon it" shall appear, and all human kind, "Both small and great" shall stand before Him to hear their final doom; when earth and sea, and death and hades shall return their dead to life again, "when heaven's last thunder shakes the world below;" when amidst the "wreck of matter, and the crush of worlds," myriads of angels shall attend the "King Eternal," the Everlasting Judge, and Time's curtain shall fall forever, (for "Time shall be no more,") then, as in the first act of man's great drama, so in this last, shall the sternest justice harmoniously blend with infinite mercy in fixing the eternal state of every child of Adam. No mistakes will be made, no oversights committed. "He will judge the world in *righteousness* by the man whom He hath ordained," (Acts 17:31,) granting pardon to the penitent believer, and administering just punishment to the impenitent rejector of the great atoning Sacrifice. In all this there is no violence done to our sense of right and justice. "There is no unrighteousness in Him." But the Scriptures referred to are but illustrations of the uniform representation of the divine attributes throughout the entire volume of Inspiration. From the first of "Genesis" to the last of "Revelation" there is no exception, no variation in the economy of the divine government over man.

And thus it might be shown that all the attributes are harmoniously exercised as they are portrayed in the Bible whether we consult its ethical, or its historical, its political, or its prophetic portions. In fact, amidst all the diversities of personal peculiarities among the writers (and they are many); amid all the changes of times and circumstances, great as they were, there is identity of teaching on all the subjects presented in this remarkable Book—the being and attributes of Jehovah God; the fact and manner of His moral government over man; His gracious will and purposes toward His rebellious creature; man's sinful and lost and helpless condition, together with his accountability to his Sovereign for his conduct in this life, are recognized and more or less definitely stated throughout all its teachings. These doctrines permeate all these writings so palpably that no thoughtful reader can fail to discover them, or to be impressed by them, with a sense of their constancy.

The question recurs: Is it possible to account for this identity of representation of these solemn doctrines upon any other supposition than that the writers were guided by the same divine Spirit in all they have written? To account for this fact on any other supposition, would make the composition of the Bible a greater miracle than any which it records to which those who deny the Inspiration so seriously object, and which they class with superstition and falsehood—or the fabrications of wicked and designing men. And, if any assert that such a fabrication is probable, or even possible, we demand that the assertion be *sustained by fact.* Mere assertion without proof avails nothing. A parallel *example* must be furnished from the annals of the human race. I ask: What documents, ancient or modern, afford such a parallel? All the labor and research of *scientists* (?) have so far failed to find such a document. And, yet, these boastful so-called "*scientists*," neither accept nor reject any thing except upon scientific principles. "Consistency, thou art a jewel." But until a literary production parallel to our Bible has been produced, the claim that these writings were divinely inspired stands unimpeached. The parade of supposed possibilities of *fraud* in its composition, or of falsehood in the professions of its human authors is the result of ignorance and of a desire to appear learned and independent thinkers, or of a *corrupt heart* and perverted judgment.

The only *rational* conclusion is, that the writers of the Bible were what they claimed to be, the messengers of God, delivering the messages He had commanded them to deliver. The entire harmony of these writers in reference to the nature and attributes of Deity is the more remarkable when we remember that there is no formal manner, nor set terms of phraseology employed to convey their conceptions of God and His attributes. On the contrary, the references to them seem to be more of an incidental nature, growing out of the nature of the subject of discourse, or the gushings of holy poetic fervour; or the rhapsodies of prophetic vision. And what has been said above more especially of justice and mercy may be said of *all* the divine attributes. The sacred writers uniformly and continually so represent them as to show them all to be co-ordinate and harmonious.

I, therefore, again insist, that the only *rational*, and, therefore, the only scientific conclusion is, that the writers of the Bible, whoever they may have been, or whenever or wherever they may have lived, must have been under the influence of and guided by a superhuman Wisdom, viz., The Spirit of God, who is the "Creator of all things in heaven and in earth, visible and invisible."

CHAPTER VII.

THE BIBLE A UNIQUE BOOK.

EVERY production of the human mind has something within it *peculiar* to itself, something that distinguishes it from every thing else. This is no less true in letters than in arts. To say, that the Bible is a *unique* Book is to say no more, in some respects, than may be said of any other book—it is peculiar. Among all the literary productions of the world, I think it safe to say that there are no two just alike, though hundreds of them may treat of the same subject, be the production of the same age, and emerge from the same or similar environments. Differences more or less important are found everywhere, in all departments or lines of human thought and activity. To the extent to which any book differs from all other books it may be called *unique*.

But after we have allowed all that may be legitimately claimed upon this principle,

THE BIBLE IS *par excellence*, A UNIQUE BOOK.

Some of the features which mark it as such I have presented in the preceding pages, and I now propose to call attention to others of a more general if not of a more striking character. Notwithstanding the cavils and high-sounding objections of the "Higher Critics" of the day, there is abundant internal evidence that different portions of the Book were written at very different periods of time, amidst very different circumstances, political, religious and literary, some dating back almost to the origin of the human race; by men of very different degrees of ability both natural and acquired; of diverse modes of thought, and varied mental constitutions.

Just how many writers contributed to the composition of the Bible has not been determined, and perhaps never will be. But, whatever may be the number or the individual qualifications of the different writers, whenever the *authority* by which they wrote is referred to, they invariably represent themselves as simply delivering the messages that had been dictated by Jehovah, and committed to them for announcement to men. It is God speaking through or by them. He alone is their Author, and the Records are made by divine guidance. Paul has said: "All Scripture is given by inspiration of God." (I prefer this rendering.) (II Tim. 3:16.) Luke says: "Beginning at Moses and all the prophets, He (Christ) expounded unto them in *all the Scriptures*, the things concerning Himself." (Luke 24:27.) The Bible is simply the being and will of God made known to man through human agency.

How unlike any other literary production in the world this is!! How can this radical unlikeness be accounted for except upon the ground claimed, viz., that it is divine in its authorship, while no other book is?

2. The *Bible alone*, as an original Book, treats of themes of the most exalted nature, and of the profoundest interest to man. God is the prominent Being from beginning to ending. He is the only absolute, independent being in the universe, and He is the central figure in the grand panorama of all revealed truths—whether in His Word or His Providence. He is "In the beginning" represented as the Eternal Self-existing Creator of "The heavens and the earth." In the closing scenes He is represented as the Omnipotent Judge of "human kind,"

by whose decisions the eternal destiny of every human soul will be decided. O, frail, dying man, herein is made known to thee thy God, and Creator, and Judge in all the majesty of His being and perfection of His character. Devoutly read, learn and obey, for this knowledge is obtained no where else. It is here only.

3. By some it is charged that the Bible is an unscientific Book. If by this is meant that it is in no sense a treatise on the so-called sciences of modern days—Astronomy, Geology, Mathematics, etc., etc., or that it does not use the terminology of modern scientists and philosophers, it is readily and gratefully granted. And, yet, it deals with the profoundest scientific problems—Deity, Sin, Cosmogony, Humanity, Eternity; and Heaven and Hell as the eternal abodes of man; with all the interests of man for time and the eternal ages. And all the revelation and the inspiration given are developments or manifestations of the knowledge of God made to man—the unfolding as it were, of the science of Deity. A personal God, Creator and Ruler of the universe of both material and immaterial existences is the Center and

Circumference of all Revelation, natural and supernatural, the source of all divine inspiration and of all good. In all this God is making Himself known to His intelligent creature, man. All the facts, doctrines and duties given or enjoined by inspiration, together with all their conditions and consequences are but subordinate parts of this revelation. Hence, no honor is paid to the inspired writers except as they *serve* their Sovereign. They are only the agents used by the Master to make His nature and will known to man. The highest honor they ever claimed or that is any where in this Book accorded to them is that they were *His servants*. The language of these writers is: "Not unto us, not unto us, but unto thy name." "The desire of our souls is unto thy name." Divine honors are accorded only to the Most High God.

A very striking illustration of this recognition of the right of Jehovah alone to the adoration of man is found in Rev. 19:10: So glorious in appearance was the heavenly messenger sent to John on the isle of Patmos he "Fell at his feet to worship him. But he (the angel) said unto him: See thou do it not; I am thy fellow-servant, and (one) of thy brethren that have the testimony of Jesus: Worship God."

Thus it is throughout the entire volume of inspiration. No creature, however exalted, however pure, however honored of God, is any where in these writings recognized as worthy of our heart's homage. God alone, the one living and true God is to be worshipped. No hero however renowned; no ancestor however loved and honored, as a man, receives divine honor. Such homage is due to God alone. The uniform recognition is: "Thou shalt worship the Lord, thy God, and Him only shalt thou serve."

4. Another unique feature of the Bible is, that its teachings are *monotheistic* throughout. It reveals to man ONE GOD, and only One, and, so far from recognizing the existence of any other, *positively* and *persistently denies* that there is any other.

There are forcible reasons for believing that for a longer or shorter period after the *dispersion* all the nations were Monotheists. But gradually in process of time, they, as nations, lost all proper conception of this One God, and invented a plurality of gods—became Polytheists. And, while there were *individuals* who adhered to the primitive monotheism, as Enoch, Seth and Noah, still the *masses* had become Polytheists before Abraham's day. Of course, all such had become idolaters. No doubt some peoples as such departed from pure monotheism earlier and some later, and only those nations who retained a knowledge of God through the Revelation He had made to men retained the primitive monotheistic faith.

This doctrine of the ONE GOD of infinite perfection, which is persistently the teaching of the Bible, is of vast moment. Pagan nations recognized "gods many," of various degrees of power and authority, frequently meeting and consulting about mundane affairs. But the councils of the gods of the most enlightened heathen nations of antiquity were frequently discordant, and their conclaves were often occasions of acrimonious strife, while the gods and goddesses were filled with mutual envies and jealousies, often laboring to thwart each others purposes. Seldom did their Supreme god call a council that such scenes were not enacted.

And even their Supreme god was subject to the "Fates," whose decrees he could neither reverse nor resist. These Fates were inexorable and their decrees unalterable. Besides, these gods and goddesses were jealous, vindictive, deceitful and lewd beyond measure. Under such conceptions of the reigning Celestials nothing was certain but uncertainties. No wonder that wars the most cruel and unjust and coupled with the death or enslavement of the prisoners, cursed the earth; for were they not each and all the wards of some god, acting under his sanction, the only trouble being that the Fates were irresistible?

But the Biblical idea of One Supreme Ruler of the Universe gives assurance of *unity of purpose* in all cosmic operations, material or immaterial, with a restful anticipation of the final consummation of ends the most beneficent and wise. There is no caprice in His government, and He fears no rival, acknowledges no peer. On the integrity of His Word, and the stability of His throne man may build and rest their dearest hopes and highest joys without a suspicion of fear. "I am the Lord, I change not," rings out from the eternal Throne.

But whatever use we may make of it, or whatever results may flow from it, the *monotheism* of the Bible is one of its *peculiar* doctrines. This is one of the features of its *uniqueness*.

The watchword or battle-cry of the Mohammedan: "There is but One God," is derived from our Book of Inspiration.

That God is here presented to us in the three relations, or manifestations of His power and work as Father, Son and Holy Spirit, does not destroy this unity—this *oneness*. These three distinctions are in our theological nomenclature called "Persons." Whether this is the best designation available may be a question. But the Christian world has become accustomed to its use and it answers our convenience, though I believe it is, to many, misleading.

The distinct manifestation of the relation of "Son" was not fully made until His Baptism in Jordan by His "Messenger," John the Baptist, at His entrance upon His public ministry. But intimations of His coming had been given throughout the Old Testament Scriptures, in types, and prophecies, beginning in the garden of Eden and typified in the sacrifices of Abel, Noah, Abraham, the Patriarchs and all the sacrifices and offerings of the Mosaic economy; and foretold more or less distinctly by all the prophets from Moses to Malachi. Whoever will carefully compare the descriptions given in the Old Testament prophecies and types of the Messiah therein foretold—His advent into the world, His character, work and death—with the historical Jesus of Nazareth as described by the writers of the New Testament Scriptures can not fail to see the identity of the historical and the prophetical man—yet *more* than a man—beyond a reasonable doubt. All the types and prophecies of the Old Testament meet, are fulfilled in Him whose advent into the world was foretold by inspired prophets hundreds of years prior to the event.

There is no other literature in the world like this. It *stands alone*, the wonder and admiration of the devout student. Indeed, no other production approaches this in its contents, its claims and its influence over men. Its subjects are broader and grander, its influence purer and more ennobling, and its claims more exalted than any other writings whatever. *Why all this?* Simply because its Author is *divine.*

5. Likewise the Bible teaches all that we may know of humanity—all that concerns and subserves man's highest interests. God is self-

existent and eternal. All other beings are mere creatures of God, and hence, had a beginning, by His will and power. The Bible tells us *how*, and, in a certain sense, when man began to be, together with his nature and condition. And, according to its teachings, man is the direct creature of God, and was created in His "image" and "likeness," endowed with noble mental powers, and, as distinguishing him above all other terrestrial beings, was also endowed with a *moral* nature, and thereby made capable of distinguishing between right and wrong, good and evil, and, hence, a subject of moral government. It also tells us that primitive man was morally pure. He must have been happy; but by transgression of his Maker's law he fell into sin, and consequently into moral ruin.

In all this account of the first act of human drama there is nothing absurd nor puerile. The writer, "A plain unvarnished tale unfolds, nothing conceals, nothing extenuates, nor sets down aught in malice." In all its subsequent teachings concerning the race the Bible deals with the solemn problems of the human soul in its relations to God and Eternity, to heaven and to hell—eternal life and eternal death. It is true that in doing this, his mundane conditions and his physical and mental wants are frequently referred to and provision made for them, and all the trustworthy history we have of the race for about 3000 years is here given. But all these are given incidentally and as subordinate to the interests of the soul—its condition, its needs and its destiny. For the delivery of the soul from condemnation and everlasting pain it offers ample provision. And these provisions are *utterly unlike those proposed by any other system of religion or philosophy.* The plan here is the consummation of the harmony of justice and mercy. Here, "Mercy and truth are met together (are in harmony); righteousness and peace have kissed each other." And this is *the one* purpose of the Book, so far as man is concerned. Here the solemn question that has perplexed the sages of the world, "How should man be just with (before) God?" is here for ever settled. The conditions are clearly set forth. All else relating to man occupies a *very subordinate* place to this. And here alone is the problem solved—that problem which affects the eternal interests of every human being. This is *science worthy of the name.*

Whether the provisions proposed meet *all* the wants or demands of the human soul is another question, and not now under discussion. What mere man has ever analyzed the human soul so as to know all the elements and possibilities of its mysterious being? Until we are assured that this has been done it becomes us to speak with modesty concerning it. But whether they do or do not, they are such as the Bible offers. But one thing is remarkable, viz., We can not conceive of a possible condition of a soul in this life nor of a *need* of it in the life to come which is not recognized and provided for in the terms proposed here. These provisions, too, are equally suited to the needs of men of all times, all climes and of all conceivable conditions. It is a Book given to man for men, without distinctions of age or condition—given to man as man—and proposes the *one* sovereign remedy for all the ills which afflict his soul.

Whence all this? Is it purely human in its origin? If so, how does it occur that it is the *only Book* of its *kind*? the only Book that deals with these solemn questions chiefly? and deals with them so as to carry conviction of truth to the mind of the honest unbiased reader? The answer *must* be: Because this is the only book known to man which the Holy Spirit dictated for man's "Instruction in righteousness," which touches man at every point, and treats with him in regard to his dearest interests, those of his soul—*his real self*, "For what shall it profit a man if he gain the whole world and lose himself."

The things of time and sense are here regarded in their *true* light and estimated at their true value—fleeting, unsatisfactory, false in promise and perishing; and yet to all men attractive, seductive and a snare. Dealing with and addressed to man in his fallen condition as the subject of sin and all its bitter fruits in this life—toil, pain, disappointment, sorrow, disease and death; and in the life to come everlasting banishment from all that is good and desirable; and subjection to intensest pain, even to hopeless despair, and "weeping and gnashing of teeth" for ever; it proposes a means of escape from these fearful results of sin and points out the way to our *Father's house*, that "House not made with hands, eternal in the heavens,"—the *home* of the SOUL, and bids him freely enter and live for ever in bliss—at home. "I am the way, the truth and the life," says Jesus. "Look unto me, *and be ye saved.*"

The whole system presented for the accomplishment of these ends is sublime in its conception, gracious in its purposes, wonderful in its adaptations and glorious in its results. It is such as no human mind could conceive and no human power could execute or make operative. Compare all the schemes of all the sages, and how signal their failure! Whence then is this? Evidently it is of God, who has here given us knowledge of Himself, and of His will and purposes of grace toward man, through those whom He has specially called and qualified by His Spirit to the performance of this gracious work, "Oh, Israel, thou hast destroyed thyself, but in me is thy help."

CHAPTER IX.

SOME OBJECTIONS NOTICED.

TO all this various objections are raised by various classes of men. I note the following:

1. It is objected that the Biblical Cosmogony is an awkward conglomerate of various heathen mythological accounts of the creation of the universe and the origin of man. I reply: This is begging the question in the baldest manner. There is no proof of its truth. It is much more reasonable, from the various accounts of the matter, to conclude that all such accounts are corrupted traditions from this as the primeval source of information. A careful comparison of the several accounts will, I think, satisfy any candid enquirer of the reasonableness of this conclusion.

2. It is objected that the writers had false conceptions of the figure of the earth and of its relation to the solar and stellar worlds; that they regarded the earth as flat, and the sun and

siderial orbs as revolving around it as their center. That this was the opinion of the scientists down to the days of Copernicus is well attested. But I do not call to mind a single passage in the Bible which, properly understood, justifies such a claim. It is true they spake of the "*ends* of the earth," meaning its most remote portions. So do we of to-day. They also spake of the sun's rising in the east and setting in the west. So do we, even our wisest astronomers. These are forms of expression known and common to all men who have any literature, and they meet all the demands of scholarship as well as of everyday life.

As to the *form* of the earth, however, I think the Bible rather favors the idea of its rotundity. Job said (26:7): "He (God) stretcheth out the north over the empty place, and hangeth the earth upon nothing." "*As for* the earth, out of it cometh bread: and under it *is turned* up as it were fire." (28:5.) This was said by that servant of God at least 2000 years before Copernicus was born. Whether Job meant to say that the central portions of the earth were a molten mass I do not know. But certain it is that he spake of the earth as swinging in space, and thus necessarily involving its rotundity.

3. It is objected that its teachings concerning what are known as miracles are unscientific and, therefore, utterly incredible. By "miracles" we understand such a suspension of known natural laws as to necessitate the intervention of supernatural power. The very definition, therefore, excludes the idea of scientific analysis of phenomena. And there is no scientific fact more fully attested than that Jehovah has at various times and in various ways interposed to suspend the operation of the general laws which He has appointed for the government of the natural world for specific and special reasons. If the testimony of credible witnesses is worthy of credence, then by all the laws of evidence known to the civil codes of the civilized world such interference has often been exercised, the skeptic and critic to the contrary notwithstanding.

4. It is objected that there are many anachronisms in the Book which render it unworthy of credence as one of divine inspiration.

Although this objection does not so much affect the question of *inspiration* as it does that of *authenticity*, yet these so intimately involve each other, I briefly notice it here, and to this objection offer the following reflection: It is a well known and recognized law of language, that all living (spoken) languages constantly change. Many words which have held their places in the vocabulary for a longer or shorter period become obsolete and are dropped from the language while new words are invented to take their places. This law is so well known and so generally recognized I need not give instances in proof.

Besides many words that are retained are changed in their signification, often assuming the exactly opposite meaning. A familiar illustration of the latter is found in our English word "Let." When James's translation of the Bible was made "Let" meant to hinder. Now it means just the *opposite.* A recognition of this fact will, no doubt, account for all Biblical anachronisms. No one claims that we have the first copies of the Hebrew originals. But we have carefully made and preserved copies. When a word has become obsolete, from whatever cause, the copyist could not be true to his important work except by inserting the (then) modern equivalent in the place of the obsolete. Thus new words would become incorporated into the sacred Books of the Jews, who, by their frequent captivities were exposed to the influence of the language of their captors.

That post-exilic words are found in pre-exilic history is the natural result of the law above referred to. Had there been no such variations we would have reason to call it forgery.

THE END.

www.ingramcontent.com/pod-product-compliance
Lightning Source LLC
Chambersburg PA
CBHW032248080426
42735CB00008B/1057

* 9 7 8 3 3 3 7 1 8 2 2 0 5 *